Lighting the Flame of Compassion

Also by Pandit Rajmani Tigunait

Inner Quest: Yoga's Answers to Life's Questions

The Himalayan Masters: A Living Tradition

Why We Fight: Practices for Lasting Peace

At the Eleventh Hour: The Biography of Swami Rama

Swami Rama of the Himalayas: His Life and Mission

Shakti: The Power in Tantra (A Scholarly Approach)

From Death to Birth: Understanding Karma and Reincarnation

The Power of Mantra and the Mystery of Initiation

Shakti Sadhana: Steps to Samadhi
(A Translation of the Tripura Rahasya)

Seven Systems of Indian Philosophy

Audio & Video

The Spirit of the Vedas

The Spirit of the Upanishads

Pulsation of the Maha Kumbha Mela

In the Footsteps of the Sages

Living Tantra™ Series

- *Tantric Traditions and Techniques*
- *The Secret of Tantric Rituals*
- *Forbidden Tantra*
- *Tantra and Kundalini*
- *Sri Chakra: The Highest Tantric Practice*
- *Sri Vidya: The Embodiment of Tantra*

Eight Steps to Self-Transformation

Nine Steps to Disarming the Mind

Lighting the Flame of Compassion

Pandit Rajmani Tigunait, Ph.D.

HIMALAYAN INSTITUTE®
PRESS
Honesdale, Pennsylvania, USA

Himalayan Institute Press
952 Bethany Turnpike, Building 2
Honesdale, Pennsylvania 18431

09 08 07 06 05 04 6 5 4 3 2 1

2005 Second Printing

Printed in China.

Watercolor Illustrations: Roger Hill

The paper used in this publication meets the minimum requirements of American National Standard for Information Sciences—Permanence of Paper for Printed Library Materials, ANSI Z39.48-1984.

ISBN 0-89389-238-6

Introduction

T*he scriptures infuse our hearts with compassion* and respect for ourselves and all living beings by proclaiming with unshakable conviction: The soul of all living beings is one and autonomous. Through sheer will it becomes many. When we internalize this knowledge and come to know ourselves as integral to the luminous consciousness that animates all life, we become both fearless and compassionate. We recognize that we are living in the embrace of that transcendental unity that creates and sustains the splendid diversity we see around us. We are no longer a threat to others and others are no longer a threat to us.

When we do not know ourselves as integral to an intricate web of relationships sustained by cooperation and compassion, we regard ourselves as separate individuals. As long as we remain locked in this circumscribed individuality, we will feel threatened by others. To fortify our individuality, we form groups and then are bewildered when we find ourselves surrounded by potential enemies. Seeking safety and security, we amass wealth and weapons to protect ourselves from these others. Instead of recognizing our planet for what it is a life-sustaining matrix imbued with divinity we treat it as a commodity, exhausting our natural resources in an attempt to insulate ourselves with material wealth.

The solution? Rise above trivial self-identity. Know who you are and rejoice in being what you are. Discover your sacred bond, first with those who are near and dear to you, and then with the larger world, both inside and outside yourself. The technique for accomplishing this is simple: honor the life force that animates everything in this world. When you recognize the sacred link that holds you in an all-embracing net of mutuality, you will notice that your heart has begun pulsating with the experience of unity with all. You will no longer suffer from the sense of separation or involve yourself in the strife that arises from mistrust and fear.

Lighting the Flame of Compassion will help you discover the best within yourself and in the rest of humanity, for these verses flow from the heart of those who see no difference between the creator and his creation. Read them and contemplate on their meaning. When the light of these words shines in your own heart, the flame of compassion will be kindled within you and you will become a beacon to others.

ॐ असतो मा सद् गमय ।
तमसो मा ज्योतिर्गमय ।
मृत्योर्मा अमृतं गमय ॥

Vedic Invocation

Om, asato mā sad gamaya
tamaso mā jyotirgamaya
mṛtyormā amṛtaṃ gamaya

Om, lead us from the unreal to the real, lead us from darkness to light, lead us from mortality to immortality.

ॐ सह नाववतु । सह नौ भुनक्तु ।
सह वीर्यं करवावहै । तेजस्वि नावधीतमस्तु ।
मा विद्विषावहै ॥ ॐ शान्तिः शान्तिः शान्तिः

Vedic Invocation

Om, saha nāvavatu, saha nau bhunaktu
saha vīryam karavāvahai tejasvi
nāvadhītamastu mā vidviṣāvahai
Om, śāntiḥ śāntiḥ śāntiḥ

Om, protect us both, nurture us both. May we grow strong together; may our understanding shine; may we not resent each other. Om, peace, peace, peace.

सङ्गच्छध्वं संवदध्वं सं वो मनांसि जानताम् ।
देवा भागं यथा पूर्वे सञ्जानाना उपासते ॥

Rig Veda 10:191.2

saṅgacchadhvam saṃvadadhvaṃ
saṃ vo manāṃsi jānatām
devā bhāgaṃ yathā pūrve sañjānānā upāsate

May we walk together, talk together, and understand each other. Like bright beings joined in right thinking, may we share our bounty with each other.

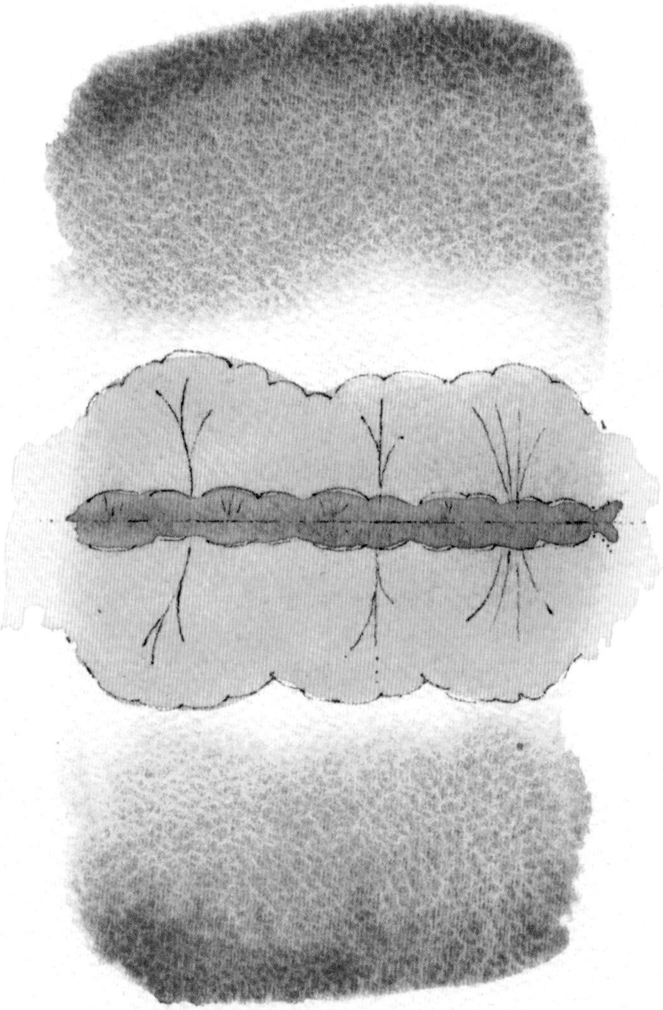

समानो मन्त्रः समितिः समानी
समानं मनः सह चित्तमेषाम् ।
समानं मन्त्रमभिमन्त्रये वः
समानेन वो हविषा जुहोमि ॥

Rig Veda 10:191.3

samāno mantraḥ samitiḥ samānī
samānaṃ manaḥ saha cittameṣām
samānam mantramabhimantraye vaḥ
samānena vo haviṣā juhomi.

May our means of protection and guidance be similar; may our communities and their assemblies share similar goals; may our minds entertain similar thoughts; may we invoke the forces of creation and offer our oblations to them with similar intent.

समानी व आकूतिः समाना हृदयानि वः ।
समानमस्तु वो मनो यथा वः सुसहासति ॥

Rig Veda 10:191.4

samānī va ākūtiḥ samānā hṛdayāni vaḥ
samānamastu vo mano yathā vaḥ susahāsati

May our actions be congruent; may our hearts be harmonious; may we be like-minded. This is how we can prosper and be truly happy.

नास्ति बुद्धिरयुक्तस्य न चायुक्तस्य भावना ।
न चाभावयतः शान्तिरशान्तस्य कुतः सुखम् ॥

Bhagavad Gita 2:66

nāsti buddhirayuktasya na
cāyuktasya bhāvanā
na cābhāvayataḥ śāntiraśāntasya
kutaḥ sukham

A person not committed to higher good is mindless. He lacks right thinking. Lacking right thinking, he is bound to be restless. How can a restless person ever be happy?

देवान्भावयतानेन ते देवा भावयन्तु वः ।
परस्परं भावयन्तः श्रेयः परमवाप्स्यथ ॥

Bhagavad Gita 3:11

devānbhāvayatānena te devā
bhāvayantu vaḥ
parasparaṃ bhāvayantaḥ śreyaḥ
paramavāpsyatha

The luminous forces of nature constantly serve you. You, too, must serve them. By serving each other selflessly, both will achieve the highest good.

अन्नाद्भवन्ति भूतानि पर्जन्यादन्नसंभवः ।
यज्ञाद्भवति पर्जन्यो यज्ञः कर्मसमुद्भवः ॥

Bhagavad Gita 3:14

annādbhavanti bhūtāni
parjanyādannasaṃbhavaḥ
yajñādbhavati parjanyo yajñaḥ
karmasamudbhavaḥ

Living beings depend on food. Food depends on rain. Rain depends on the sacred fire. The work of the sacred fire depends on action.

काम एष क्रोध एष रजोगुणसमुद्भवः ।
महाशनो महापाप्मा विद्ध्येनमिह वैरिणम् ॥

Bhagavad Gita 3:37

kāma eṣa krodha eṣa rajoguṇasamudbhavaḥ
mahāśano mahāpāpmā viddhyenam iha
vairiṇam

Desire and anger are born of inner unrest. The former has limitless appetite; the latter is the greatest of all sinners. Know that they are the real enemies.

श्वोभावा मर्त्यस्य यदन्तकैतत्
सर्वेन्द्रियाणां जरयन्ति तेजः ।
अपि सर्वं जीवितमल्पमेव
तवैव वाहास्तव नृत्यगीते ॥

Katha Upanishad 1:1.26

śvobhāvā martyasya yadantakaitat
sarvendrayāṇām jarayanti tejaḥ
api sarvam jīvitamalpameva
tavaiva vāhāstava nṛtyagīte

O Lord of Death, the teacher of living beings, all the objects of the world are short-lived. They drain our vitality. Life, and all that exists in life, is of little value [if it leads us nowhere]. Keep all the powers and pleasures of the world. [But please show me the way to live joyfully here and hereafter.]

अन्यच्छ्रेयोऽन्यदुतैव प्रेयस्ते
उभे नानार्थे पुरुषं सिनीतः ।
तयोः श्रेय आददानस्य साधु
भवति हीयतेऽर्थाद्य उ प्रेयो वृणीते ॥

Katha Upanishad 1:2.1

anyaccchreyo'nyadetaiva preyaste
ubhe nānārthe puruṣamm sinītaḥ
tayoḥ śreya ādadānasyad sādhu
bhavati hīyate'rthādya u preyo vṛṇīte

The good and the pleasant are two different things. They motivate a person to pursue different goals. The one who embraces the good meets with auspiciousness, but the one who chooses the pleasant is lost.

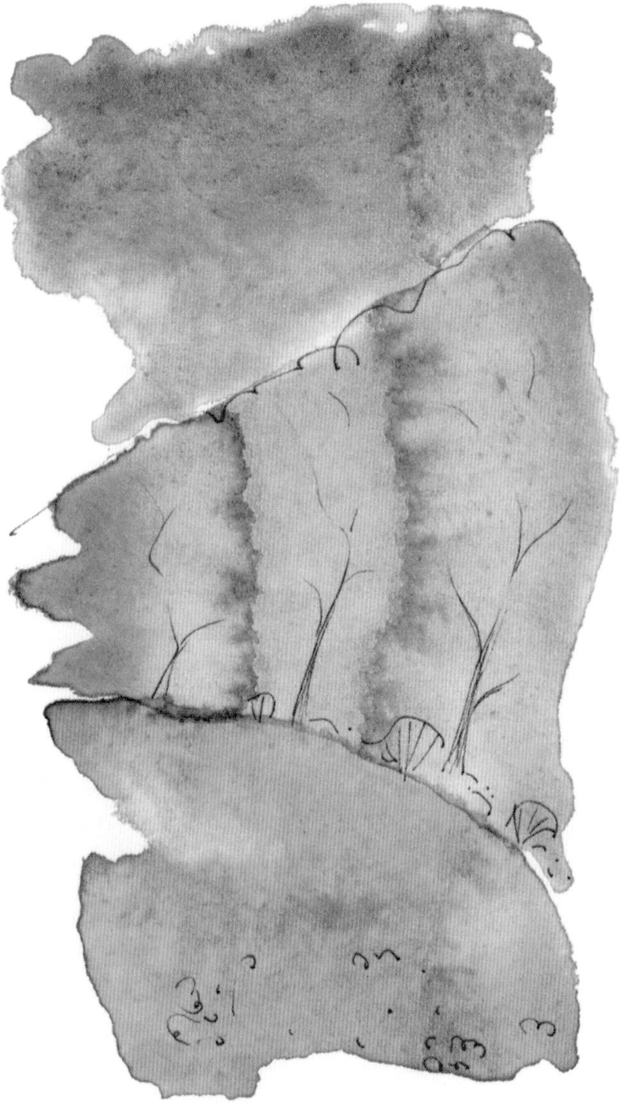

अविद्यायामन्तरे वर्तमानाः
स्वयं धीराः पण्डितंमन्यमानाः ।
दन्द्रम्यमाणाः परियन्ति मूढा
अन्धेनैव नीयमाना यथान्धाः ॥

Katha Upanishad 1:2.5

avidyāyāmantare vartamānāḥ
svayam dhīrāḥ paṇḍitaṃmanyamānāḥ
dandramyamāṇāḥ pariyanti mūḍhā
andhenaiva nīyamānā yathāndhāḥ

Dwelling in the darkness of ignorance, the ignorant believe themselves to be wise and balanced. Like the blind led by the blind, they stagger round and round.

न साम्परायः प्रतिभाति बालं
प्रमाद्यन्तं वित्तमोहेन मूढम् ।
अयं लोको नास्ति पर इति मानी
पुनः पुनर्वशमापद्यते मे ॥

Katha Upanishad 1:2.6

na sāmparāyaḥ pratibhāti bālam
pramādyantam vittamohena mūḍham
ayam loko nāsti para iti mānī
punaḥ punarvaśamāpadyate me

Those who are deluded by the charms and temptations of the world are childish and fail to comprehend the higher truth. This world is their only reality: beyond this, nothing exists. One who is convinced of this falls into the trap of birth and death again and again.

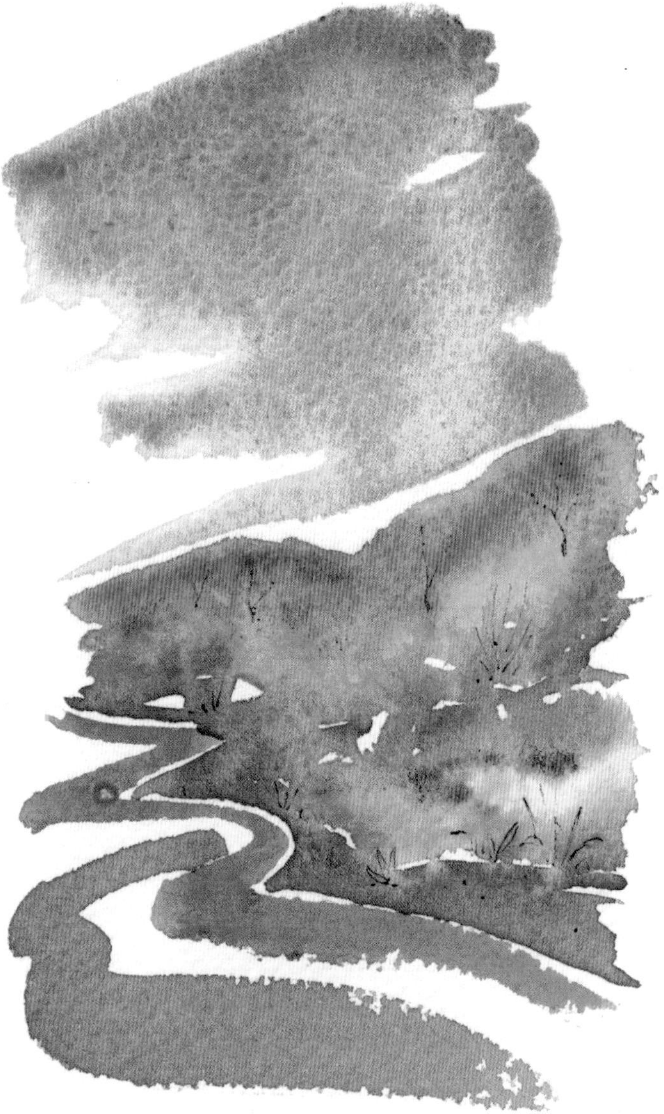

यस्त्वविज्ञानवान् भवत्ययुक्तेन मनसा सदा ।
तस्येन्द्रियाण्यवश्यानि दुष्टाश्वा इव सारथेः ॥

Katha Upanishad 1:3.5

yastvavijñānavān bhavatyayuktena
manasā sadā
tasyendriyāṇyavaśyāni duṣṭāśvā iva sāratheḥ

One who does not have right knowledge or an undisciplined mind suffers from the activities of his uncontrolled senses, just as a charioteer suffers when driving untrained horses.

यस्तु विज्ञानवान् भवति युक्तेन मनसा सदा ।
तस्येन्द्रियाणि वश्यानि सदश्वा इव सारथेः ॥

Katha Upanishad 1:3.6

yastu vijñānavān bhavati yuktena
manasā sadā
tasyendriyāṇi vaśyāni sadaśvā iva sāratheḥ

One who has right understanding and a disciplined mind enjoys controlled senses, just as a charioteer enjoys driving trained horses.

यस्त्वविज्ञानवान् भवत्यमनस्कः सदाऽशुचिः ।
न स तत् पदमाप्नोति संसारं चाधिगच्छति ॥

Katha Upanishad 1:3.7

yastvavijñānavān bhavatyamanaskaḥ
sadā'śuciḥ
na sa tat padamāpnoti saṃsāraṃ
cādhigacchati

One who does not have right understanding, whose mind is filled with thought constructs, and who lacks purity does not attain the highest realm, but remains mired in the cycle of birth and death.

यस्तु विज्ञानवान् भवति समनस्कः सदा शुचिः ।
स तु तत् पदमाप्नोति यस्माद् भूयो न जायते ॥

Katha Upanishad 1:3.8

yastu vijñānavān bhavati samanaskaḥ
sadā śuciḥ
sa tu tat padamāpnoti yasmād
bhūyo na jāyate

One who has right understanding, whose mind is free of thought constructs and who is endowed with purity, attains freedom from the snare of death and rebirth.

विज्ञानसारथिर्यस्तु मनः प्रग्रहवान् नरः ।
सोऽध्वनः पारमाप्नोति तद् विष्णोः परमं पदम् ॥

Katha Upanishad 1:3.9

vijñānasārathiryastu manaḥ
pragrahavān naraḥ
so'dhvanaḥ pāramāpnoti tad viṣṇoḥ
paramaṃ padam

One who is accompanied by right understanding and a disciplined mind completes the journey and reaches the realm of all-pervading Truth.

येन रूपं रसं गन्धं शब्दान्स्पर्शांश्च मैथुनान् ।
एतेनैव विजानाति किमत्र परिशिष्यते एतद्वै तत् ॥

Katha Upanishad 2:1.3

yena rūpaṃ rasaṃ gandhaṃ
śabdānsparśāṃśca maithunān
etenaiva vijānāti kimatra pariśiṣyate etadvai tat

If one knows this world only through taste, smell, touch, sight, hearing, and sexual pleasure, then what is there to say? It is hopeless, finished.

अङ्गुष्ठमात्रः पुरुषो मध्य आत्मनि तिष्ठति ।
ईशानो भूतभव्यस्य न ततो विजुगुप्सते एतद्वै तत् ॥

Katha Upanishad 2:1.12

aṅguṣṭamātraḥ puruṣo madhya ātmani tiṣṭati
īśāno bhūtabhavyasya na tato vijugupsate
etadvai tat

Residing in all the limbs and organs,
consciousness is seated in the core of the soul.
It is the lord of past, present, and future.
Upon knowing that Self, an aspirant is no
longer subject to confusion. This is the truth.

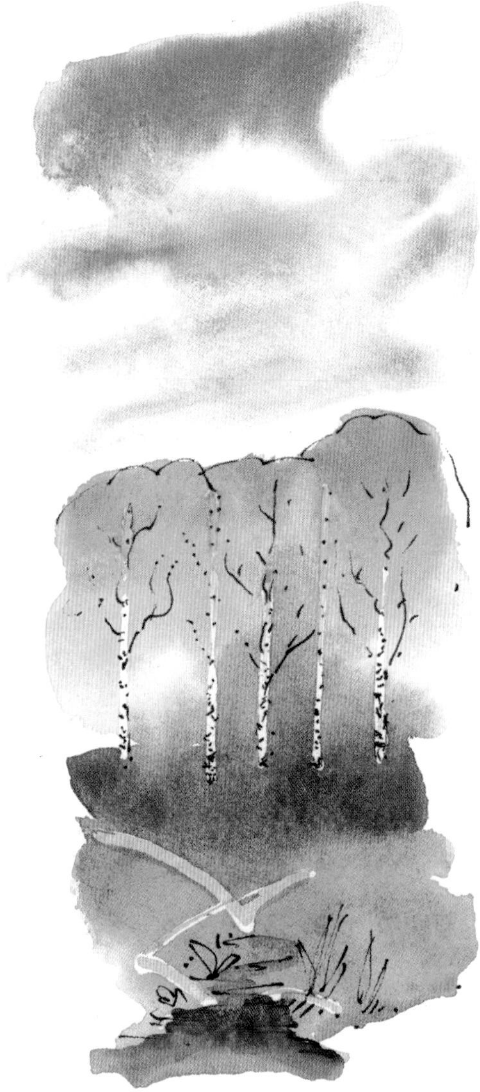

अङ्गुष्ठमात्रः पुरुषो ज्योतिरिवाधूमकः ।
ईशानो भूतभव्यस्य स एवाद्य स उ श्वः एतद्वै तत् ॥

Katha Upanishad 2:1.13

aṅguṣṭamātraḥ puruṣo jyotirivādhūmakaḥ
īśāno bhūtabhavyasya sa evādya sa u śvaḥ
etadvai tat

Residing in all the limbs and organs, consciousness is like a smokeless flame. It is the lord of past, present, and future. It exists today, and it will exist for endless tomorrows. This is the truth.

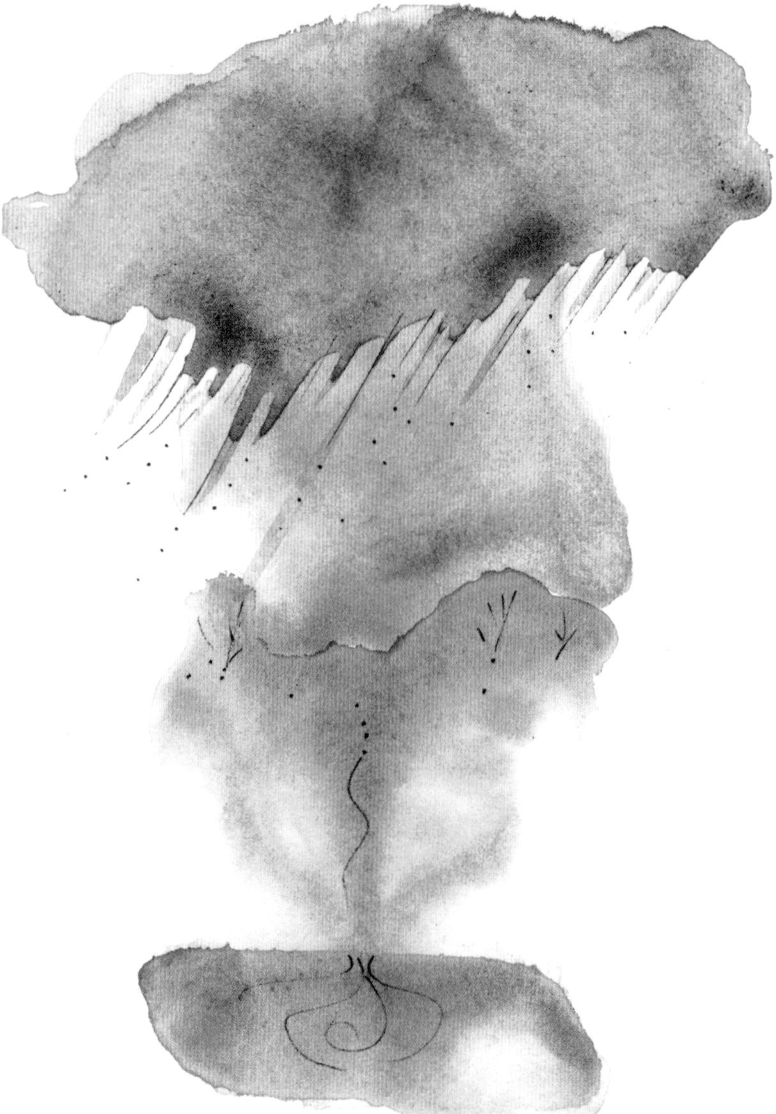

यथोदकं दुर्गे वृष्टं पर्वतेषु विधावति ।
एवं धर्मान्पृथक् पश्यंस्तानेवानुविधावति ॥

Katha Upanishad 2:1.14

yathodakaṃ durge vṛṣṭaṃ
parvateṣu vidhāvati
evaṃ dharmānpṛthak
paśyaṃstānevānuvidhāvati

Just as rain at the summit runs downhill, the seer of differences chases what he sees.

यथोदकं शुद्धे शुद्धमासिक्तं तादृगेव भवति ।
एवं मुनेर्विजानत आत्मा भवति गौतम ॥

Katha Upanishad 2:1.15

yathodakaṃ śuddhe śuddhamāsiktaṃ
tāddageva bhavati
evaṃ munervijānata ātmā bhavati gautama

Just as rain falling on pure ground remains pure, but becomes impure on impure ground, the knowledge of the Self falling in a pure heart remains pure, but becomes distorted in an impure heart.

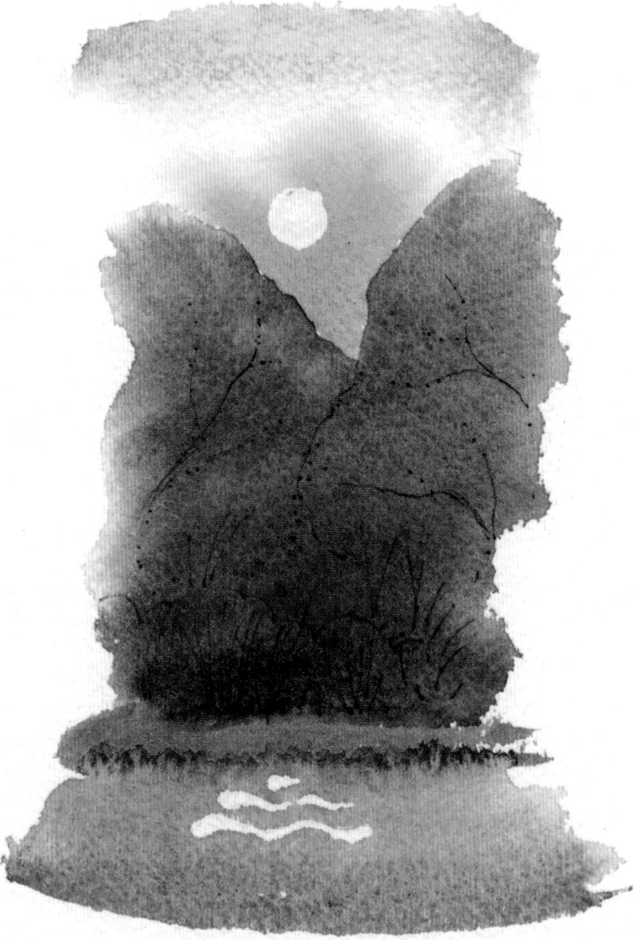

न प्राणेन नापानेन मर्त्यो जीवति कश्चन ।
इतरेण तु जीवन्ति यस्मिन्नेतावुपाश्रितौ ॥

Katha Upanishad 2:2.5

na prāṇena nāpānena martyo jīvati kaścana
itareṇa tu jīvanti yasminnetāvupāśritau

A mortal lives not by inhalation or exhalation; rather he lives by that which gives life to both inhalation and exhalation.

एको वशी सर्वभूतान्तरात्मा
एकं रूपं बहुधा यः करोति ।
तमात्मस्थं येऽनुपश्यन्ति धीराः
तेषां सुखं शाश्वतं नेतरेषाम् ॥

Katha Upanishad 2:2.12

eko vaśī sarvabhūtāntarātmā
ekaṃ rūpaṃ bahudhā yaḥ karoti
tamātmasthaṃ ye'nupaśyanti dhīrāḥ
teṣāṃ sukhaṃ śāśvataṃ netareṣāṃ

The soul of all living beings is one, and autonomous. Through sheer will, this one soul becomes many. Everlasting joy comes to those who see this one soul within, and not to anyone else.

नित्योऽनित्यानां चेतनश्चेतनानाम्
एको बहूनां यो विदधाति कामान् ।
तमात्मस्थं येऽनुपश्यन्ति धीराः
तेषां शान्तिः शाश्वती नेतरेषाम् ॥

Katha Upanishad 2:2.13

nityo'nipyānāṃ cetanaścetanānām
eko bhūnāṃ yo vidadhāti kāmān
tamātmasthaṃ ye'nupaśyanti dhīrāḥ
teṣāṃ śāntiḥ śāśvatī netareṣām

It is eternal among the eternal. It is the consciousness of consciousness. It is one among many. It is this highest being who fulfills all desires. Everlasting joy comes to those who see this consciousness within, and not to anyone else.

यदिदं किंच जगत्सर्वं प्राण एजति निःसृतम् ।
महद्भयं वज्रमुद्यतं य एतद्विदुरमृतास्ते भवन्ति ॥

Katha Upanishad 2:3.2

yadidaṃ kimca jagatsarvaṃ
prāṇa ejati niḥsṛtam
mahadbhayaṃ vajramudyataṃ
ya etadviduramṛtāste bhavanti

The life force animates everything in this world. For one who doesn't know this truth, life is full of fear, a series of calamities. But the knower of this truth is beyond death, decay, and destruction.

यदा सर्वे प्रमुच्यन्ते कामा येऽस्य हृदि श्रिताः ।
अथ मर्त्योऽमृतो भवत्यत्र ब्रह्म समश्नुते ॥

Katha Upanishad 2:3.14

yadā sarve pramucyante kāmā ye'sya hṛdi śritāḥ
atha martyo'mṛto bhavatyatra brahma samaśnute

Upon attaining freedom from all desires previously stored in one's heart, a mortal becomes immortal, and experiences oneness with the Absolute Reality here and now.

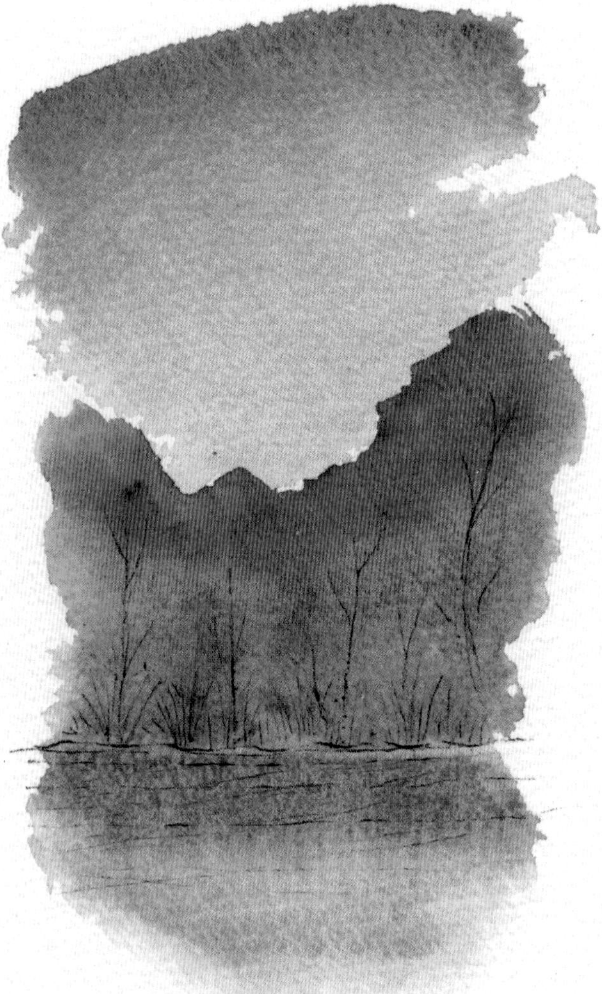

यदा सर्वे प्रभिद्यन्ते हृदयस्येह ग्रन्थयः ।
अथ मर्त्योऽमृतो भवत्येतावद्ध्यनुशासनम् ॥

Katha Upanishad 2:3.15

yadā sarve prabhidyante hṛdayasyeha
granthayaḥ
atha martyo'mṛto
bhavatyetāvaddhyanuśāsanaṃ

Upon cutting asunder all the knots in the heart, a mortal becomes immortal here and now. That is the discipline.

शतं चैका च हृदयस्य नाड्यः
तासां मूर्धानमभिनिःसृतैका ।
तयोर्ध्वमायन्नमृतत्वमेति
विष्वङ्ङन्या उत्क्रमणे भवन्ति ॥

Katha Upanishad 2:3.16

śataṃ caikā ca hṛdayasya nāḍyaḥ
tāsāṃ mūrdhānamabhiniḥ sṛtaikā
tayordhvamāyannamṛtatvameti
viṣvaṅṅanyā utkramaṇe bhavanti

Hundreds of energy channels originate from the heart. One channel goes toward the head. By making that channel move upward one is no longer subject to death, decay, and destruction. The rest of the energy channels naturally flow in every direction.

अङ्गुष्ठमात्रः पुरुषोऽन्तरात्मा
सदा जनानां हृदये संनिविष्टः ।
तं स्वाच्छरीरात्प्रवृहेन्मुञ्जादिवेषीकां धैर्येण ।
तं विद्याच्छुक्रममृतं तं विद्याच्छुक्रममृतमिति ॥

Katha Upanishad 2:3.17

aṅguṣṭhamātraḥ puruṣo'ntarātmā
sadā janānāṃ hṛdaye saṃniviṣṭaḥ
taṃ svāccharīrātpravṛhenmuñjādiveṣīkāṃ
dhairyeṇa
taṃ vidyācchukramamṛtaṃ taṃ
vidyācchukramamṛtamiti

Residing in every limb and organ, the inner Self has entered the heart of all living beings. An aspirant should patiently free this inner Self from the confines of matter and experience its boundless glory. Remember this Self is self-effulgent and immortal; upon knowing it, you are no longer subject to death, decay, and destruction.

About the Author

Pandit Rajmani Tigunait, Ph.D., the spiritual head of the Himalayan Institute®, is the successor of Swami Rama of the Himalayas. Lecturing and teaching worldwide for more than a quarter of a century, he is a regular contributor to *Yoga International* magazine and the author of twelve books, including the best-selling, *At the Eleventh Hour: The Biography of Swami Rama of the Himalayas.*

Pandit Tigunait holds two doctorates: one in Sanskrit from the University of Allahabad in India and another in Oriental Studies from the University of Pennsylvania. Family tradition gave Pandit Tigunait access to a vast range of spiritual wisdom preserved in both the written and oral traditions. Before meeting his master, Pandit Tigunait studied Sanskrit, the language of the ancient scriptures of India, as well as the languages of the Buddhist, Jaina, and Zorastrian traditions. In 1976, Swami Rama ordained Pandit Tigunait into the 5,000-year-old lineage of the Himalayan masters.

The Himalayan Institute®

The main building of the Institute headquarters near Honesdale, Pennsylvania.

A LEADER IN THE FIELD OF YOGA, meditation, spirituality, and holistic health, the Himalayan Institute® was founded by Swami Rama of the, Himalayas. The mission of the Himalayan Institute® is Swami Rama's mission—to discover and embrace the sacred link,the spirit of human heritage that unites East and West, spirituality and science, and ancient wisdom and modern technology. Using time-tested techniques of yoga, ayurveda, integrative medicine, principles of spirituality, and holistic health, the Institute has brought health, happiness, peace, and prosperity to the lives of tens of thousands for more than a quarter of a century. At the Himalayan Institute® you will learn techniques to develop a healthy body, a clear mind, and a joyful spirit, bringing a qualitative change within and without.

The Himalayan Institute's headquarters is located on a beautiful 400-acre campus in the rolling hills of the Pocono Mountains of northeastern Pennsylvania. In the spiritually vibrant atmosphere of the Institute you will meet students and seekers from all walks of life who are participating in programs in hatha yoga, meditation, stress reduction, ayurveda, nutrition, spirituality, and Eastern philosophy. Choose from weekend or weeklong seminars, monthlong self-transformation programs, longer residential programs, spiritual retreats, and custom-designed holistic health services, pancha karma, and rejuvenation programs. In the peaceful setting of the Institute, you will relax and discover the best of yourself. We invite you to join us in the ongoing process of personal growth and development.

Swami Rama transplanted his Himalayan cave to the Poconos in the form of the Himalayan Institute®. The wisdom you will find at the Institute will direct you to the safe, secure, peaceful, and joyful cave in your own heart.

> "Knowledge of various paths leads you to form your own conviction. The more you know, the more you decide to learn."
>
> —Swami Rama

PROGRAMS AND SERVICES INCLUDE:

- Weekend or extended seminars and workshops
- Meditation retreats and advanced meditation instruction
- Hatha yoga teachers' training
- Residential programs for self-development
- Holistic health services and pancha karma at the Institute's Center for Health and Healing
- Spiritual excursions
- Varcho Veda® herbal products
- Himalayan Institute Press
- *Yoga International* magazine
- Sanskrit correspondence course

To request a free copy of our quarterly guide to programs, or for further information, call 800-822-4547 or 570-253-5551, write to Himalayan Institute, 952 Bethany Turnpike, Building 1, Honesdale, PA 18431, USA, or visit our website at www.HimalayanInstitute.org.

HIMALAYAN INSTITUTE®

PRESS

The Himalayan Institute Press has long been regarded as "The Resource for Holistic Living." We publish dozens of titles, as well as audio and video tapes, that offer practical methods for living harmoniously and achieving inner balance. Our approach addresses the whole person—body, mind, and spirit—integrating the latest scientific knowledge with ancient healing and self-development techniques.

As such, we offer a wide array of titles on physical and psychological health and well-being, spiritual growth through meditation and other yogic practices, as well as translations of yogic scriptures.

Our yoga accessories include the Japa Kit for meditation practice and the Neti Pot™, the ideal tool for sinus and allergy sufferers. The Varcho Veda® line of quality herbal extracts is now available to enhance balanced health and well-being.

Subscriptions are available to a bimonthly magazine, *Yoga International*, which offers thought-provoking articles on all aspects of meditation and yoga, including yoga's sister science, ayurveda.

For a free catalog call 800-822-4547 or 570-253-5551, e-mail hibooks@HimalayanInstitute.org, fax 570-647-1552, write to Himalayan Institute Press, 630 Main St., Ste. 350, Honesdale, PA 18431-1843, USA, or visit our website at www.HimalayanInstitute.org.